The English Bulldog in the Family: Get to Know Their Unique Personality

THE ENGLISH BULLDOG IN THE FAMILY

First edition. March 13, 2024.

ISBN: 979-8223045953

Written by Gonzalo Estrada.

Table of Contents

Contents

Chapter 1: Introduction to Race

Discover the origins and characteristics of the English Bulldog, a unique and fascinating dog breed.

The English Bulldog, with its unmistakable appearance and charming personality, is one of the most popular and beloved dog breeds in the world. Originally from England, this sturdy and adorable companion has captured the hearts of many pet owners with its uniqueness.

The origins of the English Bulldog go back to ancient times. Although their precise ancestry is debated, their lineage is believed to include ancient war dogs used in the practice of boxing against bulls. Over the centuries, this breed evolved and adapted to become the English Bulldog we know today.

One of the most outstanding characteristics of this breed is its distinctive physical appearance. The English Bulldog has a large, wide head, with pronounced wrinkles and a unique facial expression. Strong jaws and powerful teeth are characteristic features of this breed. In addition, its muscular and compact body, combined with its loose and wrinkled skin, give it an impressive and at the same time tender appearance.

Despite its robust appearance, the English Bulldog is known for being a dog with a gentle and loving temperament. They make great family companions and get along especially well with children, making them the ideal choice for homes with young children. Their friendly character and loyalty to their loved ones make them an invaluable addition to any family.

However, it is important to note that the English Bulldog has specific needs that must be addressed to ensure their well-being. Because of its particular anatomy, it is prone to respiratory problems and to being overweight. A proper diet and regular exercise are critical to keeping you fit and healthy. In addition, your facial wrinkles should be cleaned and dried regularly to prevent infections and irritations.

Despite the challenges associated with their health, the love and devotion that an English Bulldog can provide to their family is incomparable. They are extremely affectionate and affectionate dogs, willing to do anything to please their owners. Their unique personality, which combines tenderness with a touch of courage, makes them loyal and trustworthy companions.

In the next chapter, we'll further explore the character and temperament of the English Bulldog, as well as some practical tips for its care and training. We invite you to continue discovering the fascinating history and peculiarities of this wonderful dog breed.

Learning about the history and characteristics of the English Bulldog is just the beginning of our exploration of this wonderful dog breed. In this second half of the chapter, we'll dive even deeper into their character and temperament, as well as some practical tips for their care and training.

One of the qualities that distinguishes the English Bulldog is its calm and friendly character. Although they can be somewhat stubborn dogs at times, in general they are loyal, affectionate and are always willing to please their owners. They are excellent family companions and tend to get along very well with other animals if properly introduced to them as puppies. However, because of their protective nature, they can be reserved with strangers, making them good guard dogs.

It is important to note that the English Bulldog requires special care due to its particular anatomy. As we mentioned earlier, they are prone to respiratory problems and to being overweight. For this reason, it is essential to provide them with a balanced diet and to control their weight. It is recommended to use high quality croquettes, adapted to the needs of the breed. It is also advisable to divide your daily ration into several small meals to avoid gastric dilatation or stomach torsion, common problems in broad-chested dogs.

In addition to taking care of your diet, it's important to pay attention to the hygiene and cleanliness of your skin and facial wrinkles. English Bulldog wrinkles can accumulate moisture and dirt, which can lead to infections and irritations. It is recommended to clean and dry wrinkles regularly, using damp wipes or a soft cloth. It is also essential to keep them cool in hot weather, as they are usually sensitive to high temperatures due to their respiratory structure.

When it comes to training, the English Bulldog can be a bit stubborn at times, so positive reinforcement and patience are key. It is advisable to start your training from an early age, using positive training techniques and rewards. These dogs respond very well to praise and treats, so it's important to use them as incentives during training sessions.

In addition to basic training, early socialization is essential for the English Bulldog. Exposing him to different situations, people and animals as a puppy will help him develop appropriate social skills. In this way, it will become a balanced and confident dog, capable of enjoying different experiences without showing any signs of aggression or fear.

In short, the English Bulldog is a unique and fascinating dog breed, full of qualities that make them ideal dogs for families. Their loving personality and unparalleled loyalty make them wonderful companions, willing to give all their love and devotion to their owners. However, like any other breed, it requires specific attention and care to ensure its well-being. With proper nutrition, cleansing of its wrinkles and early socialization, the English Bulldog will become a special member of any household.

We have reached the end of this chapter of introduction to the English Bulldog breed. I hope you have enjoyed learning more about this wonderful dog breed and that it has aroused your interest in discovering more information about them. In the next few chapters, we'll further explore some specific aspects of caring for and raising English Bulldogs, providing you with practical and useful tips to ensure their happiness and well-being in your home. Continue to discover with us the fascinating personality and peculiarities of this incredible dog breed!

Chapter 2: Choosing the English Bulldog as a pet

Evaluate if the English Bulldog is the right choice for you and your family, considering their personality and special needs.

When choosing a pet, it is important to carefully analyze the characteristics and needs of the breed that we want to add to our family. In the case of the English Bulldog, we are dealing with a species with a unique personality and special needs that we must take into account to ensure that it is the right option for us.

The charming personality of the English Bulldog is one of its main attractions. These dogs are known for being loyal, affectionate and very friendly. They always seek to be close to their owners, offering unparalleled company and unconditional love. Their affectionate nature makes them perfect for families who want to have a pet to accompany them in all their activities and provide a strong and deep bond.

However, it's also crucial to consider the special needs of this breed. English Bulldogs are brachycephalic dogs, meaning they have a flat snout and a peculiar facial structure. This can make it difficult for them to regulate their body temperature and breathe, especially in hot weather or intense exercise. Therefore, it is essential to provide them with a cool environment and to avoid strenuous activities that could put their health at risk.

In addition, English Bulldogs are known for being low-energy dogs. They're happy having moderate periods of activity and then resting peacefully next to you on the couch. This feature makes them ideal for families who don't have much time or space for long walks or intense exercise. However, it is essential to provide them with enough mental stimulation and interactive games to keep their minds active and avoid boredom.

Another aspect to consider is the special care required for wrinkled skin and short hair. English Bulldogs need regular grooming to keep their skin healthy and prevent infections. In addition, your facial wrinkles must be cleaned and dried properly to avoid moisture accumulation, which could lead to dermatological problems.

If you're considering an English Bulldog as a pet, it's crucial that you take the time to research, learn and prepare to provide all the specific needs this breed requires. Consulting with vets who specialize in English Bulldogs can go a long way to making sure you're ready for this unique experience.

In short, the English Bulldog is an exceptional pet with a charming personality, but we must be aware of its special needs before making the decision to include it in our family. Evaluate if you have the capacity to provide them with the care and attention they require. In the second half of this chapter, we'll dive into additional aspects to help you make an informed decision. Keep reading and discover more about the wonderful world of English Bulldogs!

Once you've carefully evaluated whether the English Bulldog is the right choice for you and your family, it's important to consider other aspects before making a final decision.

One of the things to consider is the space available in your home. Although English Bulldogs aren't dogs that require a lot of physical exercise, they still need a comfortable place to live. Make sure you have enough space for them to move and rest properly. It's also important to consider if you live in a house with a yard or in an apartment without access to green areas. Remember that these furry friends are not fans of extreme heat and can suffer if they are exposed to high temperatures for extended periods.

Another aspect to consider is the time you have available to dedicate to your pet. English Bulldogs are sociable dogs that enjoy spending time with their family. If you have a busy lifestyle, you may need to reconsider whether you can provide them with enough care and love. They benefit greatly from interaction and play with their loved ones. Also, remember that these dogs need to make regular visits to the vet to monitor their health and ensure that they maintain their overall well-being.

In addition, it's important to consider the financial cost of keeping an English Bulldog as a pet. Because of the special needs of this breed, veterinary and care expenses may be higher compared to other dog breeds. For example, they may require additional dental care because of the shape of their jaw and their clenched teeth. They may also be more prone to skin problems and allergies, involving additional medical treatments. Make sure you're prepared to bear these costs before making the decision to add an English Bulldog to your family.

Last but not least, it's essential to educate yourself about the potential health problems that English Bulldogs may be prone to. This breed has a genetic predisposition to certain health problems, such as hip dysplasia, respiratory problems, and eye problems. By being aware of these conditions, you can watch for signs of illness and provide them with appropriate medical care if necessary. Remember that your pet's health and well-being should always be a priority.

In conclusion, before making the decision to add an English Bulldog to your family, it is essential to carefully consider all of the aspects mentioned above. Evaluate your lifestyle, your financial resources, the time you can dedicate to it and the space available in your home. If you decide to move forward, you'll be well on your way to enjoying a loyal, loving, and unique pet. However, remember that owning an English Bulldog means taking responsibility and committing to their special care. Enjoy the second half of this chapter and keep learning about the wonderful world of English Bulldogs!

Chapter 3: Preparing for the arrival of the English Bulldog

Learn the best methods to ensure a safe and comfortable environment for your new member of the canine family.

When you decide to bring a new canine member into your home, it's important to take all necessary steps to ensure that their arrival is as comfortable and safe as possible. In the case of the English Bulldog, a breed known for its unique personality, it is essential to prepare the right environment for its well-being. In this chapter, we'll give you some tips and recommendations to ensure a successful transition for your new four-legged friend.

The first step in preparing for the arrival of your English Bulldog is to make sure you have all the essentials it will need. Don't forget to get a comfortable bed or pillow where you can rest, as well as bowls for your food and fresh water. This type of dog usually has difficulty regulating their body temperature, so you should also consider having a cool, ventilated and draft-free area for their rest.

In addition, it is essential to ensure the safety of your English Bulldog in the family environment. This breed is prone to obesity, and therefore, it's important to create a proper exercise routine to keep them in good physical shape. Don't forget to have interactive toys that provide mental stimulation and fun. It is also advisable to secure outdoor spaces with fences or meshes to prevent them from escaping, as they tend to have a greater tendency to explore their environment.

Another crucial aspect of preparing for the arrival of your English Bulldog is training and socialization. Although they are known for being friendly and affectionate dogs, it's important to educate them properly from the start. Invite your friends and family to visit so that your dog can get used to different people. This will help avoid shyness or aggressive behavior toward strangers.

In addition, socialization with other dogs from an early age is essential for the balanced development of your English Bulldog. Organizing meetings with other pet owners, preferably with well-balanced, adult dogs, can help your puppy get used to different canine personalities.

Don't forget the importance of establishing a routine for your English Bulldog. These dogs tend to be extremely loyal and enjoy predictability. Setting regular times for feeding, exercising and playing time will help your pet feel safe and comfortable in their new home.

In short, preparing for the arrival of an English Bulldog involves taking into account several aspects that are fundamental to their well-being. Make sure you have the essentials, such as a comfortable bed and bowls for your food. It provides a safe and comfortable environment, considering its sensitivity to temperature. Don't forget about the importance of socialization and early training, establishing a routine to ensure your emotional stability. Your English Bulldog will thank you!

A crucial part of preparing for the arrival of your English Bulldog is creating a safe environment at home. Be sure to remove any dangerous or toxic objects within reach of your dog. This includes cleaning products, poisonous plants, or foods that may be harmful to your health. In addition, it's important to ensure that electrical cables are out of reach, as English Bulldogs are known for chewing everything they find.

Another important aspect to consider is training your English Bulldog. These dogs are intelligent and highly trainable, so it's critical to establish clear and consistent rules from the start. Teaching him basic commands such as "sitting", "who you" or "lying down" will help establish effective communication and strengthen the relationship between you and your pet. Remember to positively reward their good behavior with praise, caresses, or small treats.

In addition to basic training, you may want to consider enrolling your English Bulldog in obedience classes or group socialization sessions. This will allow him to interact with other dogs and learn important social skills. It's also a great way to strengthen the bond with your dog and help them develop healthy trust.

Food is another fundamental aspect to ensure the well-being of your English Bulldog. These dogs have a tendency to obesity, so it is important to provide them with a balanced diet and to control their food intake. Consult your veterinarian to determine the right amount of food and opt for high-quality foods that meet their nutritional needs.

Caring for their fur also requires special attention. English Bulldogs have a short, dense coat, which can be prone to dirt accumulation and allergies. Brushing your coat regularly will help prevent knots and keep your skin healthy. In addition, you should pay attention to cleaning facial wrinkles characteristic of the breed, as they can accumulate dirt and moisture, which could cause skin infections. Gently wipe your wrinkles with a damp cloth and be sure to dry them completely.

Finally, don't forget to schedule regular visits to the vet. English Bulldogs are prone to certain health conditions, such as respiratory problems, allergies, or hip dysplasia. A specialized veterinarian will be able to monitor your health and provide you with specific recommendations for your care.

In summary, the second half of this chapter focuses on the importance of creating a safe environment, getting proper training, providing balanced nutrition, caring for the coat, and scheduling regular veterinary visits to keep your English Bulldog healthy and happy. By implementing these tips, you'll be prepared to welcome your new member to the canine family and ensure a successful coexistence. Enjoy this wonderful experience with your English Bulldog!

Chapter 4: Socialization of the English Bulldog

Discover the importance of socializing your English Bulldog from an early age to encourage balanced and friendly behavior.

Socialization is a fundamental aspect of raising an English Bulldog. Ever since they are puppies, these adorable and quirky dogs need to experiment and adapt to different environments, people and situations. Early socialization will not only help your English Bulldog develop a unique and friendly personality, but it will also contribute to their overall well-being.

English Bulldogs are known for being affectionate, loyal and friendly to their family. However, due to their territorial and protective nature, they may show some reserve or distrust towards unknown people or dogs if they have not been properly socialized. This is why it's crucial to begin socialization at an early age.

During their first weeks of life, English Bulldog puppies are completely dependent on their mother and siblings for their initial learning and development. As they grow, they enter a phase of exploration and curiosity in which they must begin to interact with other dogs and people outside their family circle. This stage is ideal for introducing them to different stimuli and situations that allow them to develop adequate social skills.

A great way to start socializing your English Bulldog is through visits from friends and family. Invite trusted people to your home so that your puppy gets used to the presence of strangers and learns to relate in a positive way. Make sure these interactions are always positive, providing rewards and praise every time your dog shows a friendly attitude.

In addition, it is essential to expose your English Bulldog to different environments and situations during their daily walks. Take him to parks, busy streets, pet stores, and other public places where he can interact with other people and dogs in a controlled manner. This gradual exposure will allow you to gain confidence and overcome potential fears or insecurities.

It's important to note that socialization isn't just about interacting with other dogs and people, but also about providing enriching experiences. Exposing your English Bulldog to different sounds, smells, textures and sensory stimuli in general will contribute to their emotional and mental development. You can use interactive toys, car rides, or even obedience classes to provide him with new experiences.

Remember that every dog is unique and their rate of socialization may vary. Some English Bulldogs may feel more comfortable in quiet environments and will gradually adapt to more challenging situations, while others may be naturally extroverted and enjoy interacting with other dogs and people from the start. Pay attention to signs of stress or discomfort that your dog may show and adjust the pace of socialization accordingly.

In short, early socialization is essential to make your English Bulldog a balanced, friendly and self-confident dog. The puppy period offers a valuable window of opportunity to shape their behavior and ensure that they feel comfortable in different environments. Remember, however, that this is only the beginning of our journey and there is much more to discover in the second part of this chapter. Stay tuned and be prepared to continue learning about the socialization of the English Bulldog. During the socialization of the English Bulldog, it is important to consider some key aspects to ensure a positive and enriching experience for your pet. Next, I'll provide you with some additional tips and recommendations to complement what we've already discussed in the first part of this chapter.

First of all, it's essential to teach your English Bulldog to socialize properly and respectfully with other dogs. Organizing controlled games and encounters with other friendly-tempered canines can help you learn social skills and establish positive relationships. During these interactions, watch your dog's communication signals closely and make sure he's comfortable at all times. If you notice any signs of discomfort or aggression, remove your dog from the situation and seek help from a canine behavior professional.

In addition to socializing with other dogs, your English Bulldog must also learn to interact appropriately with people. It encourages positive encounters with different individuals, including adults and children of all ages. Teach your children and other people how to interact properly with your dog, explaining that they should approach them in a gentle and respectful way, avoiding sudden or intimidating movements. Remember that English Bulldogs are very sensitive dogs, so it's essential that interactions are always friendly and positive.

Another important facet of English Bulldog socialization is exposure to different stimuli and environments. As your puppy grows, take him to different places and allow him to experience varied situations. For example, take your dog for a walk in the car to get used to traveling and moving around. Also, visit different places with it, such as parks, beaches or even pet-friendly cafes and restaurants. This gradual and controlled exposure will allow your English Bulldog to become confident and comfortable in any environment.

Don't forget that socialization should not only focus on outside activities, but also at home. Establish clear and consistent routines so that your dog feels safe and understands what are acceptable behaviors. Spend time teaching him basic obedience commands and positively reinforce his good behavior with praise and rewards.

Remember that every English Bulldog is unique and may have different socialization needs. Some may be more shy or reserved, while others may be more outgoing and looking for constant interactions.

It's important to respect your dog's individual rhythm and adapt socialization according to their personality and comfort.

In conclusion, socialization is a fundamental aspect in raising a balanced and friendly English Bulldog. Through exposure to different people, dogs, environments and stimuli, you'll help your pet develop appropriate social skills and feel comfortable in any situation. Remember to be patient, understanding and persistent in this process, as the benefits of proper socialization will last a lifetime for your English Bulldog.

Keep reading and enjoy the journey of discovering the socialization of the English Bulldog! In the second part of this chapter, we'll explore some additional socialization strategies and I'll share stories and advice from other English Bulldog owners with you. Stay tuned and get ready to keep learning about this wonderful dog breed!

Chapter 5: Basic Training for the English Bulldog

Learn techniques and practical tips to educate your English Bulldog and establish a good relationship based on mutual respect.

The best way to begin basic training for your English Bulldog is to understand their unique personality. These adorable dogs are known for their calm and friendly nature, making them great companions for the whole family. However, their inherent stubbornness can make the training process somewhat difficult. But don't worry! With patience, consistency and love, you can successfully educate your English Bulldog.

It's important to remember that training must be based on positive reinforcement. Make sure to reward your dog every time he performs a desired action, such as sitting down, coming when you call him, or relieving himself in the right place. You can use treats, verbal praise, or even caresses to motivate him and let him know that he has done something right. Avoid physical punishment or the use of negative training techniques, as this will only create fear and confusion in your Bulldog.

One of the first commands you should teach your English Bulldog is to sit down. This is critical to establishing control and obedience. Start with a place that's quiet and free from distractions. Hold a treat close to its snout and move it upward while clearly saying the word "feel". The dog will need to follow the treat with its eyes and will naturally sit down. The moment it happens, immediately reward it and repeat the process several times a day. With constant practice, your English Bulldog will learn to sit alone before the command.

Another important command is the "come" command. This will allow you to have good control over your dog while you are away from home or during walks. Start with a long strap in an open space, such as a park. Call your Bulldog by name and clearly tell him "come" as you take a few steps back. If your dog comes to you, reward him and compliment him. If it doesn't come, don't drag it to you, as this will create a negative association. Instead, step back even further so that the dog naturally follows you, and when it does, reward it again. With practice and constant repetition, your English Bulldog will learn to come to you at all times.

These are just a few basic guidelines for training your English Bulldog, but remember that every dog is unique and may require different approaches. It's essential to have patience, be consistent, and always use positive reinforcement. In addition, training is not limited to just basic commands. You can also teach him fun tricks such as screwing up, going around or picking up objects. This will strengthen the bond between you and your Bulldog and keep him mentally stimulated.

Read on in the second part of this chapter to discover more tips and techniques for basic training your English Bulldog! I am very excited to share with you the second half of this chapter on basic training for the English Bulldog. In the first part, I explained to you the importance of understanding your Bulldog's unique personality and how to use positive reinforcement to teach him commands such as "sit" and "come". Now, let's continue with more useful tips and techniques.

A fundamental aspect of training your English Bulldog is to establish clear limits from the start. It's important to define the house rules and make sure you understand them. This will help avoid undesirable behavior, such as biting furniture, stealing food, or jumping on people. Always remember that your dog needs to know what to expect from him and what behaviors are acceptable.

One of the best ways to set limits is to use the "ignore and reward" technique. If your Bulldog commits an unwanted action, such as biting an inappropriate object, simply ignore it and don't pay attention to it. Then, when he takes a positive action, such as playing with his toy or staying calm, reward and praise him. This technique will teach your dog that negative behaviors don't attract attention, while positive behaviors do.

Another important command to teach your English Bulldog is "still" or "still". This is especially useful for those times when you need your dog to calm down, such as when you're getting visitors or when you're busy around the house. To teach him this command, start by clearly saying the word "still" and show him a treat. Compliment your dog when he stays still and reward him with the treat. Repeat this in different situations until your Bulldog can stay still for longer periods of time.

In addition to basic commands, it's also important to teach your English Bulldog to properly socialize with other dogs and people. Early socialization is key to keeping your dog comfortable and confident in different situations. Take him for walks to busy places, organize meetings with other dogs and allow him to interact with different people. Remember to reward and praise your dog for his good behavior during these social experiences.

Don't forget that training isn't just about teaching commands, it's also about strengthening the bond and communication between you and your English Bulldog. Spend time playing with him, caressing him, and talking to him in a soft, friendly voice. This will help build a strong relationship based on mutual trust and affection.

To end this chapter, I want to remind you that every English Bulldog is unique and can learn at their own pace. Some dogs may need more time and patience than others, and that's okay. The most important thing is to be consistent, set clear limits, and always use positive reinforcement.

I hope this chapter has provided you with useful tips and techniques for basic training your English Bulldog. Remember that patience and love are key throughout the process. Enjoy every moment of training and watch your dog learn and grow!

Chapter 6: Care and Feeding of the English Bulldog

Learn how to provide a balanced diet and the care necessary to keep your English Bulldog healthy and happy.

When we decide to share our home with a dog, we take responsibility for providing them with a full and healthy life. In the specific case of the English Bulldog, one of the most beloved and popular breeds, it is essential to take into account certain special care both in its diet and in its general well-being. In this chapter, we'll give you valuable tips and recommendations so you can provide everything you need.

A balanced diet is essential to keep your English Bulldog in optimal health. These adorable canines have a tendency to gain weight easily, so it's crucial to control their portions and provide them with a balanced diet. Opting for a quality food, designed specifically for your breed and stage of life, is an excellent choice. These foods usually contain the nutrients necessary for their development and well-being, thus avoiding deficiencies or excesses that could harm them.

Remember that every English Bulldog is unique, so it's important to adapt the amount of food according to their age, activity level and metabolism. Consulting with a veterinary specialist will allow you to determine the appropriate portions for your pet and thus avoid problems of overweight or obesity, which can lead to long-term health complications.

In addition to nutrition, physical care is another essential aspect of keeping your English Bulldog happy and healthy. Its short, bushy coat requires regular brushing to remove dead hair and prevent knots from forming. In addition, the characteristic wrinkles on your face should be gently and regularly cleaned, using specific products recommended by your veterinarian. This way, you can prevent skin infections and keep your skin in good condition.

The eyes and ears are other areas that require special attention. The folds around the eyes should be inspected regularly to avoid irritation or accumulation of secretions. Use specific products to gently clean them, following your veterinarian's instructions. As for the ears, remember to clean them gently, removing the visible earwax on the outside without going too far into the ear canal, as it could cause damage.

When it comes to exercise, the English Bulldog is not a particularly active breed. However, it's important to provide him with the opportunity for daily physical activity, even if only moderately. Short walks and interactive games are ideal for keeping you in shape and stimulating your mind. Avoid exposing it to extreme weather conditions, as its physiognomy can make it difficult to breathe.

In short, providing a balanced diet and the necessary care is essential to keeping your English Bulldog healthy and happy. Be sure to consult a veterinarian who specializes in caring for this breed for accurate guidance adapted to the individual needs of your canine companion.

Learn how to provide a balanced diet and the care necessary to keep your English Bulldog healthy and happy.

In the second half of this chapter, we will focus on other important aspects of English Bulldog care and nutrition. In addition to providing, you with a balanced diet, it's crucial to pay attention to your dental and mental health.

Dental hygiene is essential to avoid dental problems and diseases in our canine companions. English Bulldogs, like many other breeds, are prone to developing periodontal disease, due to their facial and jaw structure. To keep your teeth and gums healthy, it is advisable to brush your teeth regularly with products that are appropriate for dogs. You can also choose special dental toys to help clean your teeth while you play.

In addition, it's important to pay attention to their mental health and boost their intelligence. Although English Bulldogs are known for being quiet and well adapted to living indoors, they still need mental stimulation to avoid boredom. Puzzle games and interactive toys can help keep your mind active and avoid unwanted behavior, such as excessive barking or destroying furniture.

Regular bathing is also necessary to keep your English Bulldog clean and healthy. However, keep in mind that excessive bathing can remove natural oils from your skin and cause dryness. Consult your veterinarian about the appropriate frequency of baths, as well as the recommended cleaning products for their skin and coat.

In addition, it is essential to pay attention to the health problems common to this breed. Hip dysplasia and respiratory problems are conditions to which English Bulldogs are more susceptible. Regular veterinary checkups will detect any health problems at an early stage and take the necessary steps to care for them.

Don't forget to provide them with a safe environment suitable for their well-being. English Bulldogs are sensitive to high temperatures and may have difficulty regulating their body temperature. Therefore, it's important to provide them with a cool, well-ventilated space, especially during the warmer months.

When it comes to rest, English Bulldogs are known for being good sleepyheads. Make sure you provide them with a comfortable and quiet bed where they can rest properly. Remember that rest is essential for your health and vitality.

In conclusion, caring for and feeding your English Bulldog properly is not only important for their physical health, but also for their overall well-being. By providing him with a balanced diet, taking care of his hygiene and health, stimulating him mentally and providing him with a safe and adequate environment, you will be guaranteeing a full and happy life for your faithful companion.

Always remember to consult a veterinarian specialized in the breed for specific guidance adapted to the individual needs of your English Bulldog.

Chapter 7: English Bulldog Health

L earn about the main health concerns that may affect your English Bulldog and how to prevent or properly address them.

When you decide to integrate an English Bulldog into your family, it's essential that you consider any potential health concerns that may affect this breed. Although English Bulldogs are known for their friendly character and rugged appearance, like any other breed, they also face certain specific health conditions that may require special attention and care.

One of the main health concerns you should know about is hip dysplasia, a condition that affects the joints of these adorable canines. Hip dysplasia can limit their mobility and cause pain. If you notice that your English Bulldog seems to have difficulty getting up or walking, it's important to see your trusted veterinarian to make a proper diagnosis and explore treatment options, such as physical therapy or surgery, if necessary.

Another common health concern in these dogs is Bulldog facial dermatitis, also known as "acneic dermatitis". This condition is characterized by pimples and rashes on the skin of the English Bulldog's snout and chin. These dermatological problems can be due to a variety of causes, such as allergies, bacteria, or genetic factors. If you notice signs of facial dermatitis in your Bulldog, it's critical that we schedule a visit to the vet to determine the best treatment plan and prevent potential complications.

In addition, we must take into account the predisposition of the English Bulldog to suffer from respiratory problems. Their physical shape, with a large head and a truncated lower jaw, can hinder their ability to breathe properly. This condition, known as brachycephalic syndrome, can lead to episodes of respiratory distress, snoring, and increased sensitivity to heat. As responsible guardians of our beloved English Bulldogs, we must provide them with a cool environment, avoid intense exercise on hot days, and regularly go to the vet to monitor their respiratory health.

Obesity is another major concern that we must consider when caring for our English Bulldog. These dogs have a tendency to gain weight easily, which can aggravate potential health problems. It's essential to keep them at an adequate weight through a balanced diet and regular exercise. Consult your veterinarian about the most appropriate feeding regime for your Bulldog, based on their age, activity level and individual needs.

These are just a few of the major health concerns affecting English Bulldogs. As you go deeper into caring for your Bulldog, you'll discover other specific conditions and considerations. The key to ensuring a healthy life for your pet is early detection and regular medical care. Never hesitate to seek the advice of veterinary professionals to ensure the well-being and happiness of your beloved English Bulldog.

Throughout this chapter, we've discussed some of the major health concerns that can affect your English Bulldog. However, it's important to remember that every dog is unique and may face different health issues. We will now address some additional considerations for the care and prevention of your Bulldog's health.

One of the common conditions affecting English Bulldogs is sensitivity to heat. Because of their facial structure, these dogs have difficulty regulating their body temperature in hot weather. They can suffer from heat stroke quickly if they are not provided with a cool, ventilated environment. It's essential to ensure that your Bulldog has access to shade and fresh water at all times, especially during hot days. Avoid taking them out for walks during the hottest hours and watch for signs of heat exhaustion, such as excessive panting, lethargy, and pale gums. If you suspect that your Bulldog is suffering from heat stroke, seek immediate veterinary attention.

In addition, you should pay attention to the oral health of your English Bulldog. This breed is prone to dental problems, such as plaque and tartar build-up, as well as periodontal disease. Lack of regular dental care can lead to tooth loss and mouth infections that can affect your pet's overall health. Therefore, it is recommended to brush your Bulldog's teeth regularly and take him to the vet for professional dental cleanings as needed.

Another important consideration is the care of your English Bulldog's skin and coat. Because of the breed's characteristic facial and body folds, these dogs are prone to skin infections and dermatological problems. It is essential to keep the folds clean and dry, preventing the accumulation of moisture and dirt. Clean the folds of your Bulldog regularly with special products to prevent the proliferation of bacteria. In addition, regular brushing of the coat will help keep it clean and tangle-free.

Finally, we can't forget the importance of keeping your English Bulldog at a healthy weight. A proper diet and regular exercise are critical to preventing obesity and maintaining your pet's health. Consult your veterinarian to determine the right amount and type of food for your dog, as well as to establish an appropriate exercise plan. It's important to remember that Bulldogs are a low-energy breed, so exercise should be moderate and adapted to their individual needs.

In short, taking care of your English Bulldog's health requires special attention and care. From joint concerns to dental care and weight management, there are many important considerations to consider. The key is prevention, constant monitoring and regular veterinary care.

Remember that your English Bulldog trusts you to keep him healthy and happy. Being informed about the specific health concerns of this breed and taking the necessary steps to address them will ensure a long and full life for your beloved canine companion.

Continue to educate yourself and always seek the advice of veterinary professionals to provide the best possible care for your English Bulldog. Your pet will thank you!

Chapter 8: The Unique Personality of the English Bulldog

The English Bulldog is a dog breed known for its distinctive and charming personality. Its unique and friendly character makes it a wonderful life companion for many families and pet owners. In this chapter, we'll explore the characteristics that make the English Bulldog a special dog, and how these qualities influence its interaction with the family and other animals.

One of the most outstanding characteristics of the English Bulldog is its calm and relaxed nature. Unlike other dog breeds that are energetic and active, this friendly canine prefers to spend his time resting and enjoying the company of his family. Their easy-going personality makes them an excellent choice for homes with quieter rhythms of life.

In addition to its serenity, the English Bulldog is known for its unwavering loyalty to its family. They are extremely affectionate dogs and are constantly seeking the attention and affection of those around them. If you're looking for a loyal and loving companion, the English Bulldog may be the perfect choice.

Another unique trait of this breed is its ability to adapt to different family types and environments. Despite their impressive appearance, they are very sociable dogs and enjoy the company of children and adults alike. Because of their friendly nature, they are excellent for living with other animals if they are taught properly as puppies. Their patience and tolerance make them ideal companions for homes that already have other pets.

However, although the English Bulldog is known for being a calm, affectionate and adaptable dog, it also has some peculiarities in its personality. One of the aspects that we must mention is their stubbornness. Sometimes, they can be stubborn and have their own idea of how things should be. This requires a patient and consistent owner who can set clear boundaries and provide adequate leadership.

In addition, due to their unique facial structure, English Bulldogs may experience some respiratory challenges. This can result in excessive snoring and shortness of breath during intense exercise or in extreme temperatures. Taking care of their health and providing them with a cool, well-ventilated environment is essential to ensure their well-being.

By learning about these distinctive characteristics of the English Bulldog's personality, we can better understand how they relate to their experience in the family and their interaction with other animals. Their relaxed character, loyalty and adaptability make them a popular choice for many families. However, it's important to remember that every dog is unique and can vary in personality and temperament.

One of the English Bulldog's most notable qualities is its willingness to be a great companion and protector of its family. Their loyalty to household members is admirable, and they are willing to do everything in their power to keep their loved ones safe. It's no wonder they're considered excellent family dogs.

In addition to their unwavering loyalty, English Bulldogs are also known for their loving and caring nature. They are dogs that greatly enjoy human contact and seek the company of their owners at all times. Their unconditional love is one of the reasons this breed is so popular with families with children. English Bulldogs are patient and tolerant, making them excellent playmates for the little ones in the household.

Despite their impressive appearance, English Bulldogs are extremely sociable dogs and get along well with other animals if introduced properly from an early age. Their friendly and peaceful nature makes them ideal companions for homes that already have other pets. However, it's crucial to remember that every dog is unique and can present a variety of personalities and temperaments.

We should also mention that, while English Bulldogs are generally calm and relaxed dogs, they can sometimes be stubborn and have a mind of their own. Therefore, it is essential for the owner to be patient and set clear boundaries to maintain a harmonious environment in the home. Consistency in training and proper education are essential to help them develop good behaviors and avoid behavioral problems in the future.

Another important aspect to note is that English Bulldogs can face some respiratory challenges due to their unique facial structure. This can result in excessive snoring and shortness of breath during intense exercise or in extreme temperatures. To ensure their well-being, it is essential to provide them with a cool, well-ventilated environment, and to avoid situations that could endanger their respiratory health.

In short, the English Bulldog is a dog breed with a unique and charming personality. Their serenity, loyalty and adaptability make them a popular choice for many families and pet owners. However, it's important to remember that every dog is individual and can vary in personality and temperament. By understanding these distinctive characteristics, we can establish a deeper connection with our English Bulldogs and provide them with the love and care they deserve.

Remember that the English Bulldog is an animal that offers its unconditional love and friendship, but it also requires our constant attention and care. In the next chapter, we'll explore how to maintain the health and well-being of our wonderful English Bulldogs. Don't miss it!

Chapter 9: The English Bulldog and the Children

Learn how the English Bulldog can become an ideal companion for children and how to foster a safe and loving relationship between them.

Children and animals have a special connection. The presence of a pet in the home not only provides companionship, but also promotes the emotional development of the little ones. In this chapter, we'll explore how the English Bulldog can become a great friend and companion for children.

The English Bulldog is known for its gentleness and patience, making it an excellent companion for the youngest members of the family. This breed is affectionate and adapts easily to family life, including children. However, it's always important to monitor interactions between children and dogs to ensure the safety of both parties.

One of the reasons why the English Bulldog is so suitable for living with children is its calm nature. These dogs are famous for their balanced temperament and their ability to remain calm in chaotic situations. Their patience and tenderness make them an excellent playmate for children, as they gladly tolerate childhood games and tricks.

Despite its sturdy size, the English Bulldog is a friendly and gentle dog. This breed has a particularly close relationship with children and has the ability to provide them with emotional security. English Bulldogs are loyal and protective, creating a trusting environment for the little ones. Children can feel supported by having a furry friend by their side who cares for them and loves them unconditionally.

It is essential to teach children to interact respectfully with dogs, especially with an English Bulldog. Although these dogs are tolerant, it's important for children to understand how to approach and touch a dog safely. Teaching them to respect the dog's space and not to disturb him during his rest will help to maintain a harmonious relationship.

In addition to teaching children to interact properly with the English Bulldog, it is equally important to teach the dog to behave appropriately with children. Early training is essential to fostering a secure and loving relationship between both parties. Teaching your dog basic obedience commands and setting clear limits will help prevent uncomfortable or dangerous situations.

Children can actively participate in caring for the English Bulldog, which will further strengthen their bond. From helping with feeding and brushing to walking together, these activities will allow children to feel responsible and connected to their pet. In addition, they will promote respect and empathy for animals.

In short, the English Bulldog can become an ideal companion for children. Their loving nature, patience and ability to provide emotional security make this breed perfect for being part of family life. However, it is essential to teach both children and dogs to interact properly and to set clear limits. In this way, a secure and loving relationship will be fostered that will benefit both parties.

It will continue... The benefits of having an English Bulldog as a companion for children are not just limited to fun and company. This breed can also teach young children important lessons in responsibility and compassion. Here we'll explore how children can actively participate in caring for their English Bulldog and further strengthen their bond.

One of the easiest ways children can get involved in caring for their English Bulldog is by helping with feeding. Children can be responsible for measuring and serving the dog's food, always under adult supervision, and ensuring that it has fresh, available water at all times. This task will not only promote children's responsibility, but it will also allow them to understand the importance of proper nutrition for the dog's health.

Another way children can get involved is by helping with the English Bulldog's brushing. Although this breed doesn't require frequent brushing, it's important to keep their fur clean and tangle-free. Children can learn to gently brush their dog, always respecting their comfort and avoiding causing discomfort. In addition, this activity will strengthen the bond between the child and the dog, as both will enjoy moments of care and mutual attention.

The rides also provide an excellent opportunity for children to get involved in caring for their English Bulldog. Under adult supervision, children can hold on to the leash and walk alongside the dog. This will not only provide exercise and mental stimulation for both of you, but it will also allow you to enjoy the outdoors and strengthen your connection.

In addition to daily tasks, it's important for children to also understand the importance of setting clear limits for their English Bulldog. Teaching the dog basic obedience commands, such as sitting, standing still, or pawing, will not only help maintain a safe environment, but it will also allow children to feel more secure and in control when interacting with the dog. This will teach both of them to communicate and understand each other, promoting a relationship of respect and trust.

Finally, it is essential to promote a compassionate and empathetic attitude towards animals in children. Teaching them to treat the English Bulldog with kindness and respect, to recognize its needs and not to use it as a toy, is essential for a peaceful and loving coexistence. Children must understand that dogs also have emotions and need their space and rest.

In conclusion, having an English Bulldog as a companion for children can be a wonderful experience. The benefits this breed brings to family life are countless, from companionship and fun to important lessons in responsibility and compassion. However, it is essential that both the children and the dog learn to interact appropriately and set clear limits. In this way, a strong and loving relationship will be built that will last a lifetime.

Chapter 10: The English Bulldog and Other Animals

L earn how to introduce your English Bulldog to other animals at home and how to promote peaceful and harmonious coexistence.

The process of introducing a new furry member to your home can be exciting and full of adventure. If you already have an English Bulldog and are considering adding another animal to your family, it is important to take certain precautions to ensure that the presentation is done properly and a peaceful and harmonious coexistence is encouraged.

Before bringing a new four-legged friend home, it's essential to consider the personality of your English Bulldog. Although these dogs are known for their calm and friendly disposition, each Bulldog is unique and may have different reactions to the presence of another animal. Watch how your Bulldog interacts with other dogs or animals in the park or in controlled situations. This will give you a clear idea of how you might react to the arrival of a new partner.

Once you've chosen the new member of your family, it's important to make a gradual introduction. Don't rush or force the situation, as this could create stress for both your Bulldog and the new animal. It starts with short, supervised presentations, in a neutral place such as a nearby park. Keep both animals on a leash to have greater control of the situation and avoid putting them together in small spaces at first.

During these first interactions, watch your English Bulldog's reactions closely. Look for signs of tension or aggression, such as lifting the hair on your back, grunting, or looking upright. If you notice any signs of discomfort, stop the interaction and try again at a later time. It is important to remember that each animal has its own rhythm and it is necessary to respect its individual limits.

As interactions become more positive and calmer, it's time to start bringing the new partner home. Prepare ahead of time, providing a separate place for each animal, with separate food, water and toys. This will help reduce rivalry for resources and provide a safe space for everyone to relax. It is advisable to maintain an established routine for both animals, as the structure and clear rules will provide them with security and emotional stability.

Remember to reward and praise your Bulldog when he shows a desired behavior during the interaction with the new animal. These positive reinforcements will help to reinforce their good behavior and to promote peaceful coexistence. Patience and consistency are key during this process, as it can take time for both your Bulldog and the new animal to get used to each other.

In conclusion, introducing your English Bulldog to other animals at home requires a gradual and careful approach. Observe the personality of your Bulldog, make supervised presentations and provide individual spaces for each of the animals. Remember to positively reinforce appropriate behaviors and be patient throughout the process. Peaceful and harmonious coexistence between your English Bulldog and other animals is possible with dedication and love!

After having made the initial presentations in a neutral space, it's time to take the new animal home and begin to establish coexistence between your English Bulldog and him. During this stage, it is important to remember that each animal has its own pace of adaptation, so it is essential to have patience and be consistent in the process.

Once at home, make sure each animal has its own individual space to rest and eat. Providing them with separate beds, different food and water bowls, as well as toys and a place where they can relax, will allow everyone to feel safe and secure. This will help reduce any chance of conflict due to resource rivalry.

It is essential to establish an established routine for both animals. A regular eating schedule, daily walks and moments of play together will help to strengthen the bonds between them and to establish a harmonious coexistence. The English Bulldog is an affectionate and sociable dog, so it's important to make sure you spend quality time with him and provide him with care and affection.

During interactions between your English Bulldog and the new animal, it's essential to pay attention to their reactions and communicate with them in a calm and empathetic manner. If you notice any signs of discomfort or tension, stop the interaction and try again later. Remember that each animal has its own adaptation process and it is necessary to respect their individual limits.

In addition to supervised interactions, it's important to provide quiet time and individual rest for both animals. Establishing spaces where everyone can retire and relax without interruption will help reduce any possible stress and promote a peaceful environment.

During this introduction process, remember to positively reinforce your English Bulldog's good behavior. Use praise, caresses and prizes when you are calm and friendly with the new animal. This positive reinforcement will help to strengthen their good behavior and promote a harmonious coexistence.

As time goes on, it's likely that your English Bulldog and the new animal will begin to establish their own dynamics and build a positive relationship between them. However, it's important to remember that this process takes time and dedication. Don't be discouraged if there are challenges or moments of tension at first, keep working on the introduction and fostering an environment of respect and calm.

In conclusion, introducing a new animal to your home can be an exciting yet challenging process. With patience, attention and dedication, it is possible to achieve a peaceful and harmonious coexistence between your English Bulldog and other animals. Remember to respect the rate of adaptation of each animal, provide individual spaces and positively reinforce appropriate behaviors. With love and care, your home will become a place where all members of your family, including your pets, feel loved and in harmony.

Chapter 11: The English Bulldog and the Daily Routine

Discover how to establish a balanced and satisfying routine for your English Bulldog, ensuring their physical and emotional well-being.

English Bulldogs are wonderful dogs that provide their owners with unique company. Their friendly personality and rugged appearance make them a popular choice as pets in many families. However, as a breed with certain special needs, it is essential to establish a daily routine that meets both their physical and emotional needs.

The daily routine is essential for the English Bulldog's well-being, as it provides them with structure and stability. Starting the day with a morning walk is a great way to allow them to release energy accumulated during the night. These walks not only provide physical exercise, but they also stimulate their senses, allowing them to explore the environment and enjoy new experiences.

After the walk, it's important to spend time feeding your English Bulldog. This breed tends to have problems with being overweight, so it's crucial to provide them with a balanced diet and to control their food intake. Consult your veterinarian to ensure that the diet is adapted to the specific needs of your English Bulldog.

Once your pet has eaten, it's time to consider their daily hygiene. English Bulldogs have distinctive facial folds that require regular care to prevent infections and keep their skin healthy. Gently clean these folds using products recommended by your veterinarian and be sure to dry them properly. Also, don't forget to brush their fur to prevent the accumulation of loose hair and keep it clean and free of knots.

After hygiene, it's the perfect time to provide them with time for play and socialization. English Bulldogs are very social animals that enjoy the company of their family and other dogs. Organize some fun activities, such as search games or interaction with interactive toys, that stimulate their minds and allow them to exercise their natural instincts.

In addition to the game, you should also consider training your English Bulldog. These dogs are intelligent and respond well to positive reinforcement techniques. Spend time teaching them basic commands, such as sitting, staying, and coming when called. This will not only strengthen the bond between you and your pet, but it will also provide them with mental stimulation and satisfy their need to learn.

Last but not least, give your English Bulldog time to rest. Although they are energetic dogs, they also need to sleep and recharge. Make sure you provide them with a comfortable and quiet place where they can rest without being interrupted. A good night's sleep is essential for your physical and emotional health.

Establishing a balanced and satisfying daily routine for your English Bulldog is not only beneficial for them, but also for you as a pet owner. It will help you to have a happy and healthy dog, which will be reflected in their behavior and in the quality of life of the whole family. Continue reading the second part of this chapter to discover more tips and recommendations for maintaining an effective and exciting routine for your beloved English Bulldog.

After a day full of activities and care, it's important to make sure your English Bulldog has adequate rest time. Like humans, dogs also need rest to recover energy and maintain their physical and emotional well-being.

Find a quiet and comfortable place where your English Bulldog can rest undisturbed. Make sure you provide them with a bed or a soft, cozy area where they can relax. This will help them feel safe and secure, allowing them to rest properly.

During the night, it is advisable to establish a regular sleep schedule for your English Bulldog. Try to maintain a consistent routine so that your pet gets used to bedtime and feels calmer during the night. This can also help prevent sleep-related behavioral problems, such as separation anxiety.

Remember that adequate sleep is essential for the health of your English Bulldog. During sleep, your body repairs itself and your immune system is strengthened. In addition, adequate rest also influences your mood and energy level the next day. So, make sure you provide them with an environment that is conducive to a restful sleep.

Maintain a regular feeding routine for your English Bulldog. They need to receive their meals at set times to avoid overweight problems and maintain a healthy digestive system. Consult your veterinarian to determine the right amount of food and specific feeding schedules for your pet.

In addition to food and rest, play and socialization time is also essential to the well-being of your English Bulldog. Organize times in the day to interact with them and provide them with opportunities to socialize with other dogs and people. This will help them stay mentally stimulated and happy.

Consider different gaming activities that are suitable for your English Bulldog. You can try interactive toys that challenge them mentally, or play search games that keep them physically active. Be sure to adapt activities to their individual needs, taking into account their age and energy level.

Finally, don't forget that continuous training is key to maintaining a satisfying daily routine for your English Bulldog. Spend time teaching them new commands and positively reinforce their good behavior. This will not only strengthen their bond with you, but it will also provide them with a sense of accomplishment and satisfaction.

With a balanced and satisfying daily routine, your English Bulldog can enjoy a healthy and happy life. By providing them with structure and stability in their daily lives, you will ensure their physical and emotional well-being. Remember to adapt the routine to your pet's individual needs and be aware of any changes in their behavior or health.

We hope these tips will help you establish a perfect routine for your beloved English Bulldog! By following these steps, you can enjoy a successful coexistence full of unforgettable moments with your faithful companion. Don't miss the next part of this chapter, where we'll give you even more recommendations to ensure your English Bulldog's happiness and well-being!

Chapter 12: Physical Activity and Entertainment for the English Bulldog

Learn about the exercise and entertainment needs of the English Bulldog, and how to provide him with fun activities to keep him active and enrich his life.

The English Bulldog is a friendly and loving breed that tends to be quite calm compared to other dogs. However, this doesn't mean that we shouldn't pay attention to their need for physical activity and entertainment. Although it may seem like they prefer to spend their time dozing on the couch, it's important to remember that all dogs, including the English Bulldog, need regular exercise to stay healthy and happy.

The physical and mental health of your English Bulldog depends largely on the amount of exercise and stimulation we provide. If they are not given the opportunity to burn energy and be distracted, they may begin to develop behavioral problems or even suffer from obesity. Therefore, it's crucial to find the right balance between rest and activity.

The first thing to keep in mind is that the English Bulldog is not an athletic dog breed and doesn't need intense exercise routines like other, more energetic dogs. Instead, they benefit from daily walks at a moderate pace, preferably at less hot times of the day. This allows them to stretch their legs, explore their environment and socialize with other dogs.

In addition to walks, there are other fun ways to keep your English Bulldog active and entertained. Fetch and bring games are a great way to stimulate your mind and encourage your hunting instinct. You can use interactive toys or special balls designed for dogs, throwing the object and encouraging your English Bulldog to recover it.

Another option is to practice obedience and training games that will not only provide you with physical exercise, but will also strengthen the bond between you and your dog. English Bulldogs are intelligent and respond well to commands when taught in a positive way and by rewarding them with treats or words of encouragement. You can practice basic commands such as sitting, standing still, pulling up, and others.

When it comes to entertainment, puzzle toys and teethers are great options to keep your English Bulldog busy and mentally stimulated. These challenging toys provide them with a task to solve, such as finding a hidden treat or releasing a prize. This not only keeps them entertained, but it also helps them exercise their jaws and teeth.

Remember, the goal is to keep your English Bulldog active and to enrich their life in a fun and accessible way. Don't forget to consider the physical limitations of this breed and consult with your veterinarian about the most appropriate activities for your dog. In the second part of this chapter, we'll explore more entertainment options and give you tips to keep your English Bulldog happy and satisfied. Stay tuned, the fun is about to continue!

In addition to rides and fetch and bring games, there are other physical and entertainment activities you can offer your English Bulldog to keep him active and happy. One popular option is swimming, as this breed tends to be prone to respiratory problems due to its unique facial structure. Not only does swimming provide them with low-impact exercise, it also helps to strengthen their muscles and joints, without putting too much strain on their respiratory system. However, it's important to remember that not all English bulldogs enjoy water, so it's essential to gradually introduce this activity and make sure they feel comfortable and safe in the water.

Another fun option is agility, a dog sport that involves crossing obstacles and performing certain exercises on a circuit. Although English bulldogs may not be the fastest or most agile dogs, they can enjoy this activity as long as it suits their individual needs and abilities. You can set up a circuit in your garden with some simple obstacles, such as tunnels, low jumps, and walkways. As your English Bulldog gains confidence and skill, you can add more challenges. Always remember to reward and praise your dog for his achievements, even if he doesn't achieve perfection.

In addition to these physical activities, it's also important to provide mental stimulation to your English Bulldog. Interactive toys and puzzles for dogs are great options to keep your mind active and avoid boredom. These toys usually contain compartments and hiding places where you can hide treats or prizes for your dog to discover. This not only gives them mental stimulation, but it also keeps them entertained and satisfied. You can try different types of toys to find out which ones your English Bulldog likes best, whether those that require movement or those that must solve a problem.

Socialization is also critical to the well-being of your English Bulldog. Although they tend to be friendly and sociable, it's important to expose them to different situations, people, and other dogs from an early age. You can organize visits to dog parks or meet up with friends who have well-behaved dogs. This will allow them to socialize, play and learn to behave appropriately in different environments and situations.

Finally, remember that safety should always be a priority when providing physical activity and entertainment for your English Bulldog. Be sure to monitor him at all times, especially during outdoor activities, to avoid accidents and injuries. Also, consider the weather conditions, avoiding exercising during the hottest hours and making sure they always have access to fresh water and shade.

In short, exercise and entertainment are fundamental aspects in the life of an English Bulldog. Providing them with fun and stimulating activities helps them not only to stay active and fit, but also to promote their mental and emotional well-being. From walks appropriate to your energy level to fetch and bring games, swimming, agility, interactive toys and socialization, there are plenty of options to keep your English

Bulldog happy and healthy. Remember to adapt activities to your dog's individual needs and always check with your veterinarian for specific recommendations. Enjoy your time together and don't forget to celebrate every small achievement of your beloved English Bulldog!

Chapter 13: The English Bulldog and Veterinary Visits

Get information and advice on how to manage veterinary visits and ensure the health and well-being of your English Bulldog.

Visits to the vet are an essential part of caring for your English Bulldog. While these visits can create some anxiety for both your pet and you, it's important to understand that they are necessary to ensure their long-term health and well-being.

Before taking your English Bulldog to the vet, it is recommended that you inform yourself about the basic care you must provide. This includes keeping her immunization schedule up to date, making sure she has a balanced diet appropriate for her age and health, and providing her with enough exercise and mental stimulation.

During a visit to the vet, your English Bulldog may experience stress and anxiety due to factors such as an unfamiliar environment, different smells and sounds, and the presence of other pets. It's essential that you prepare beforehand to minimize these negative effects and make the experience as smooth as possible for your furry companion.

One way to reduce stress is to accustom your English Bulldog to carriers or transport cages from an early age. These devices provide safety and protection during travel and visits to the vet. Also, be sure to bring a familiar blanket or toy to provide them with some comfort during the waiting time.

When you arrive at the veterinary clinic, stay calm and show confidence to your English Bulldog. Dogs can sense their owners' nervousness, so it's important to provide them with security and peace of mind. Also, be patient during the wait time, as vets are often busy and your shift can take a while.

During the consultation, it is essential that you provide detailed information about the symptoms or any changes in the behavior of your English Bulldog. This will help the veterinarian to make an accurate diagnosis and provide appropriate treatment. Don't forget to mention any changes in your diet, elimination habits, or physical activity.

Also, take the opportunity to address any concerns or questions you may have about caring for your English Bulldog. Veterinarians are there to help and advise you on everything related to the health and well-being of your pet. Ask about preventive measures you can take, such as regular deworming, and the specific care your English Bulldog may need depending on their age and condition.

Remember that visits to the vet are an essential part of the commitment you make when you have an English Bulldog as part of your family. These reviews make it possible to identify health problems at an early stage and treat them in a timely manner, increasing the chances of successful recovery.

Just as you take care of your English Bulldog at home, the support and experience of a professional veterinarian are essential to ensure that your pet lives a long and healthy life. Don't skimp on resources when it comes to their well-being, as your English Bulldog will depend on you to receive the right care.

In the next chapter, we will continue to explore different aspects related to the health and well-being of your English Bulldog. We will learn more tips for their daily care and we will delve into how to prevent different diseases to which they are prone. Don't miss it!

During your consultation with your veterinarian, it's important to follow these recommendations to ensure a successful and satisfactory visit for both your English Bulldog and you.

First, try to stay calm and calm during the veterinary exam. Your dog can easily detect your emotions, so it's essential to convey security and confidence. This will help him feel more comfortable and relaxed during the process.

During the physical exam, the veterinarian will check different aspects of your English Bulldog's health, such as its temperature, heart rate, gum density and color, and joint mobility. If you have any particular concerns, be sure to mention them so that the vet can pay special attention to that area.

In addition to the physical exam, the veterinarian may perform additional tests, such as blood tests, x-rays, or ultrasound, to obtain more accurate information about your English Bulldog's health. These tests can help detect health problems at an early stage and facilitate appropriate and timely treatment.

During your consultation, take the opportunity to ask questions and get advice about the daily care of your English Bulldog. Veterinarians are there to advise you and answer all your concerns. Ask about the right food for your dog, exercise needs, dental care, and any other questions you may have.

Also, talk to your vet about preventive measures you can take to ensure the health of your English Bulldog. This can include regular deworming, appropriate vaccinations, and regular health checks.

Remember that communication between you and your vet is key to optimal care for your English Bulldog. Always be honest and provide all relevant information about your pet's health and behavior. This will help the veterinarian to make a more accurate diagnosis and provide appropriate treatment.

Before you finish your appointment, make sure you get all the necessary information about the recommended treatment for your English Bulldog. Ask about medication doses, length of treatment, and any side effects you should be aware of.

Once the consultation is over, it is important to follow the veterinarian's recommendations for the ongoing care of your English Bulldog at home. This can include giving medication as prescribed, providing you with adequate nutrition, providing you with regular exercise, and making sure you have a safe and clean environment.

Remember that a visit to the vet is a fundamental step in caring for the health and well-being of your English Bulldog. Don't skimp on resources or on finding the best medical care for your pet. Your English Bulldog trusts you to ensure their well-being, and the support of a professional veterinarian is essential to achieve this.

In the next chapter of this book, we'll explore more practical tips for the daily care of your English Bulldog, as well as preventive measures to avoid common diseases. Don't miss out on this valuable information that will help you keep your pet healthy and happy.

Chapter 14: The English Bulldog and the Changing Environment

Learn how to help your English Bulldog adapt to changing environments and how to minimize stress during challenging situations.

English Bulldogs are known for their unique and charming personality. They are loyal and loving dogs that often become an inseparable part of the family. However, like any other pet, English Bulldogs can also face challenges when it comes to adapting to changes in their environment.

Our furry friends can be quite sensitive to changes in their daily routine or in the environment around them. A move to a new home, the arrival of a baby, the presence of other animals or simply a change in the family routine can create stress for our beloved English Bulldogs.

It's important to note that these changes can significantly affect your behavior and well-being. That's why, in this chapter, we'll explore practical tips to help your English Bulldog adapt to these situations, thus minimizing the stress they may experience.

The main key to making it easier for your English Bulldog to adapt is patience and unconditional love. Understanding that the adaptation process takes time and that each dog has its own pace is essential. Don't expect your English Bulldog to instantly adjust to a new environment or to a change in their routine. Give him time to explore and familiarize himself with his new space.

An effective way to help your English Bulldog adapt to a new environment is to maintain consistency in the daily routine. Although you may be tempted to change things because of changes in your life, it's important to continue to maintain a set structure and schedule for your dog. This will provide a sense of security and predictability, which is especially important during times of change.

Another aspect to consider is the gradual introduction of new stimuli and situations. If you're adding a new member to the family, such as a baby, it's a good idea to introduce yourself in a calm and controlled manner. Let your English Bulldog approach the new member in a gradual and supervised way, making sure to provide him with enough time to get used to this new family dynamic.

In challenging situations such as a visit to the vet or a car trip, it's important to minimize stress as much as possible. You can familiarize your English Bulldog with these situations by making regular visits to the vet or taking him on short trips by car from an early age. This will help your dog feel more comfortable and secure in these scenarios.

Also, remember to give your English Bulldog their own space where they feel safe and protected. You can create a quiet and cozy area in your home, equipped with a comfortable bed and favorite toys. This will give your dog a shelter he can go to when he needs to relax and rest.

In the second half of this chapter, we'll explore additional strategies to help your English Bulldog better adapt to changing environments, along with practical tips for minimizing stress in challenging situations. Remember, gradual adaptation, unconditional love and patience are key to accompanying your English Bulldog in these moments of transition. Read on and discover how you can make life easier and more enjoyable for your faithful four-legged companion!

In the second half of this chapter, we'll continue to explore additional strategies to help your English Bulldog adapt to changing environments and minimize stress in challenging situations. These recommendations are based on an understanding of the specific needs and characteristics of this unique breed.

One of the keys to making it easier for your English Bulldog to adapt is proper socialization. Gradually exposing you to different people, animals and situations from an early age will help you feel more secure and confident in different environments. Organizing regular encounters with other friendly dogs and allowing them to interact with other animals under controlled supervision will help promote their ability to adapt.

It's also important to pay attention to the signs of stress your English Bulldog may show. These can include moaning, excessive panting, compulsive licking, or even destructive behavior. If you notice any of these signs, it's essential to provide him with a calm and safe environment so that he can relax and calm down. Avoid scolding or punishing him, as this will only increase his stress.

During times of change and stress, remember to maintain clear and consistent communication with your English Bulldog. Using simple and clear commands, combined with positive reinforcements, will help to establish good communication between the two. Also, be sure to maintain a calm and relaxed attitude, as dogs are very sensitive to their owners' emotions.

If you're experiencing a drastic change in your home, such as a move, you can help your English Bulldog gradually adapt. Start by allowing you to explore and familiarize yourself with a specific room or area, and then expand your access as you become more comfortable. This will give you a sense of security and allow you to adjust to the new environment more calmly.

Another useful strategy is to provide your English Bulldog with stimulating mental and physical activities. English Bulldogs are intelligent and curious, so activities such as prize hunting games, obedience training or daily walks can help keep their mind and body active. This will not only reduce your stress, but it will also strengthen the bond between the two.

Finally, remember to pay attention to your English Bulldog's diet during times of change and stress. Some dogs may lose their appetite or have digestive problems due to anxiety. Consult your veterinarian for recommendations on the right diet and consider using feeding toys to make meals more stimulating and fun.

In short, helping your English Bulldog adapt to changing environments is a process that requires patience, love and understanding. Providing him with a safe and predictable environment, adequate socialization, attention to his stress signs, clear communication and stimulating activities are some of the strategies you can implement. Always remember to check with your vet if you have any concerns or questions.

I hope these tips will be useful to accompany your faithful companion in times of transition. English Bulldogs have a unique and charming personality, and with the right care, you can help them adapt and have a happy and balanced life. Continue to enjoy the company of your English Bulldog and give him the love and support he deserves!

Chapter 15: English Bulldog Communication and Signals

Learn to interpret the English Bulldog's communication signals and to strengthen the bond between you and your pet through effective communication.

Effective communication is essential to establishing a strong bond between you and your English Bulldog. As a pet owner, it's important to understand the signs this wonderful dog uses to express and communicate with you. Throughout this chapter, we'll explore these signals and learn how to correctly interpret them.

The English Bulldog is known for being a friendly and affectionate dog breed. However, every dog has their own unique personality and it's important to learn how to communicate with them effectively to understand their needs and feelings. Proper communication will not only improve the relationship between you and your pet, but it will also ensure their well-being and happiness.

One of the English Bulldog's most obvious signs of communication is their body language. Observing their posture, movements, and facial expressions will give you clues about how they're feeling. For example, if your Bulldog is relaxed and his tail is slightly raised, he is likely to be happy and relaxed. If your tail is between your legs and your posture is hunched, you may be showing signs of fear or submission.

In addition to body language, English Bulldogs also use sounds and vocalizations to communicate. They may bark, growl, moan, or whine to express different emotions or needs. For example, a high-pitched, energetic bark can indicate excitement, while a soft growl can be a sign of discomfort or warning.

It's essential that you learn to interpret these vocal and body signals to understand the needs of your English Bulldog. This will allow you to respond appropriately and strengthen the bond between the two. When you understand what your dog is trying to communicate, you can adjust your response according to their needs and provide emotional support.

In addition to visual and vocal cues, physical contact also plays a crucial role in communicating with your English Bulldog. Just like humans, dogs enjoy physical contact and affection. Caressing their head, stroking their back, or simply being close to them strengthens the bond and provides them with security.

However, it's important to note that every English Bulldog is unique and may have individual preferences when it comes to physical contact. Some dogs may enjoy intense cuddling and petting, while others may prefer softer, more limited contact. Observe how your pet reacts to physical contact and respect personal preferences.

In short, effective communication is the key to strengthening the bond between you and your English Bulldog. Knowing and understanding the communication signals they use will allow you to understand their needs, emotions and desires in a more precise way. Observe their body language, listen to their vocalizations, and use the right physical contact to establish strong, affectionate communication.

Remember, effective communication not only benefits your English Bulldog, but also you as a pet owner. By better understanding your dog, you'll be able to meet their needs and provide them with a happy and safe environment. In the second half of this chapter, we'll delve into specific techniques to further strengthen communication with your English Bulldog. You're about to discover exciting strategies that will help you establish a stronger and deeper connection with your beloved pet. Get ready to be surprised! The second half of this chapter will focus on specific techniques to further strengthen communication with your English Bulldog. These exciting strategies will help you establish a stronger and deeper connection with your beloved pet. Get ready to be surprised!

One of the most powerful tools you can use to effectively communicate with your English Bulldog is training. Training helps establish a solid foundation of communication and obedience between you and your dog. You can teach him basic commands, such as "sit", "stay" and "come", allowing him to understand your instructions and respond appropriately.

To train your English Bulldog, it's important to use positive reinforcement techniques. This involves rewarding and praising your dog when he correctly performs an action or follows a command. You can use treats, affectionate caresses, or words of praise to reinforce the desired behavior. Remember, positive reinforcement encourages positive communication and strengthens the bond between you and your pet.

In addition to training, another important technique for strengthening communication with your English Bulldog is patience. Every dog learns at their own pace and it's essential to have patience and understanding during the training process. Avoid frustration and stay positive while working with your pet. Your patience and persistence will be rewarded with positive results over time.

Another way to strengthen communication with your English Bulldog is to spend quality time together. Whether through daily walks, games or simply spending time in company, it's important to establish exclusive moments to be with your pet. This regular interaction will strengthen the bond between the two and allow you to better understand their needs and wants.

Also, take advantage of opportunities to actively communicate with your dog. Talk to him clearly and consistently, using appropriate tones of voice. Dogs are very sensitive to the tone of voice and can capture our emotions through it. Encouraging and affectionate when you are performing desirable behaviors, but firm and clear when you must correct unwanted behaviors.

It's also important to remember that non-verbal communication plays an essential role in your relationship with your English Bulldog. Use body language to give her clear and consistent messages. For example, avoid bending over or leaning over your dog, as this can be interpreted as a threatening posture. Instead, maintain a relaxed and open posture to promote an environment of trust.

In short, strengthening communication with your English Bulldog is essential to establish a strong bond between the two. Use training techniques based on positive reinforcement, be patient and spend quality time together. Act consistently both verbally and non-verbally and see your relationship with your pet improve as their communication improves.

Remember, every English Bulldog is unique and may have individual preferences when it comes to communication. Observe, listen and be sensitive to their needs to adapt your communication style to their preferences. By doing so, you can enjoy a stronger, deeper and more meaningful relationship with your beloved English Bulldog. Take this opportunity to strengthen the bond and communication with your faithful companion!

Chapter 16: The English Bulldog and Behavior Problems

Identify potential behavioral problems in your English Bulldog and learn effective strategies to correct them and encourage balanced behavior.

Pet owners know how wonderful it is to share our life with an English Bulldog. Their tenderness, loyalty and unique personality make us feel fortunate to have them as part of our family. However, as with any other pet, behavioral challenges can occur. In this chapter, we will learn to identify potential behavioral problems in English Bulldogs and how to effectively address them to achieve a harmonious coexistence.

It's important to understand that behavioral problems in dogs can have a variety of causes, such as lack of socialization, poor education, fear, stress, or even physical illness. In the same way, each English Bulldog may have different reactions and needs, so it is essential to observe and understand their behavior individually.

One of the most common behavioral problems in English Bulldogs is the tendency to chew on inappropriate objects, such as furniture, shoes or other personal items. This behavior can result from boredom, anxiety, or even dental problems. To correct this behavior, it is essential to provide them with sufficient mental and physical stimulation through interactive toys or outdoor activities. We must also ensure that we provide them with an appropriate diet and regularly check their dental health.

Another common problem is excessive barking. English Bulldogs, while generally quiet, can become noisy if they feel anxious, bored, or in need of attention. To address this behavior, it's important to identify the underlying cause and work on its resolution. Giving them enough exercise, establishing structured routines, and providing them with quiet, safe spaces can help reduce excessive barking.

Aggression can also be a problem in some English Bulldogs. It's vital to remember that aggression is not a natural or desired behavior in any dog breed. If our English Bulldog shows signs of aggression, such as grunting, showing its teeth or attempting to bite, it is essential to seek professional help from a dog trainer or ethologist. These experts will be able to evaluate the situation and provide us with the appropriate strategies to manage this behavior, always prioritizing the safety of all family members.

Fear and anxiety can also affect the behavior of our English Bulldogs. Some may be afraid of certain sounds, objects, or situations, which can lead to unwanted behavior, such as hiding, shaking, or even urinating indoors. In these cases, it is essential to work on the dog's trust and security through positive reinforcement, gradual exposure to scary situations and, in some cases, the support of an animal behavior professional.

In short, identifying and addressing behavioral problems in our English Bulldogs is essential to maintaining a balanced and harmonious coexistence. By providing them with the right care and care, as well as seeking professional help when needed, we can help our beloved furry companions overcome any challenges that come their way. In the second part of this chapter, we will address specific strategies to correct these problems and to encourage balanced behavior in our English Bulldogs. Don't miss this key information to improve the life of your faithful friend! Our English Bulldogs are faithful and loving animals, but like any other pet, they can also face behavioral challenges. In the first half of this chapter, we explored some of the most common problems, such as the tendency to chew on inappropriate objects, excessive barking, aggressiveness, and fear. Now, we will continue to explore effective strategies to correct these problems and to encourage balanced behavior in our beloved English Bulldogs.

One way to correct the tendency to chew on inappropriate objects is to provide them with a variety of interactive toys. Not only will these toys provide them with mental stimulation, but they will also help them redirect their energy from chewing forbidden objects to something more productive. Also, be sure to dedicate daily time to playing with them and taking them for outdoor walks. This will not only provide them with physical exercise, but it will also help them to release any accumulated tension.

As for excessive barking, it's important to establish structured routines and provide them with enough exercise. English Bulldogs are dogs that enjoy company and need to feel included in family life. So, make sure you dedicate quality time to them and provide them with the right social stimulus. In addition, when they are in a stressful or anxious situation, it is essential to provide them with a quiet and safe space where they can relax.

Aggression is a more serious problem and requires immediate attention. If your English Bulldog shows signs of aggression, such as grunts or attempts to bite, seek professional help from a dog trainer or ethologist. These experts will assess the situation and provide you with appropriate training strategies and techniques to manage this behavior. Remember, we must always prioritize the safety of all family members and the dog itself.

As for fear and anxiety, it is essential to work on building the dog's trust and security. Apply positive reinforcement to reward and celebrate their achievements. In addition, gradual, controlled exposure to fearful situations can help them overcome their fears. In some cases, you may need to seek the help of an animal behavior professional to specifically address your English Bulldog's phobias and anxieties.

Remember that every English Bulldog is unique and may require different approaches to correct their unwanted behavior. Take a close look at your pet and understand their individual needs. If you feel that despite your efforts you are not achieving an improvement in their behavior, don't hesitate to seek the help of a professional. These experts are trained to understand and address behavioral problems in dogs effectively.

In conclusion, our coexistence with English Bulldogs can be harmonious and balanced if we identify and effectively address their behavioral problems. Providing them with mental and physical stimulation, establishing structured routines, providing them with a safe space, and seeking professional help when needed are some of the key strategies to improve their behavior. Our beloved furry companions can overcome any challenge with our love and care. Let's keep learning and encouraging a happy and balanced life for our English Bulldogs!

Chapter 17: The English Bulldog in Society

Explore the role of the English Bulldog as a pet in society and how to promote respectful and responsible coexistence with other pet owners.

When we adopt an English Bulldog into our family, we are welcoming a loyal and loving companion. However, it is important to note that our beloved Bulldog is not only part of our life, but also of society in general. In this chapter, we'll explore the role that our beloved breed plays in society and how we can foster a harmonious coexistence with other pet owners.

English Bulldogs are known for their unique and charming personality. Their quirky appearance and adorable facial expressions make them a very popular breed among dog lovers. However, it's important to remember that not all dogs react the same way in different situations. As responsible owners, we must ensure that we understand and respect the needs and limits of our Bulldogs, as well as those of other dogs and their owners.

One of the keys to promoting respectful coexistence is the proper socialization of our English Bulldog from an early age. Exposing him to different environments, people and other dogs will help him feel more comfortable and confident in varied situations. This is crucial, as a well-socialized dog will be less likely to show aggressive behavior or fear towards other dogs or people.

In addition, it is vital to understand that each dog breed has its own specific characteristics and needs. We must always remember that our

Bulldog is not simply a pet, but a living being with particular emotions and requirements. As a breed that can face respiratory challenges, we must pay special attention to their health and well-being. This includes providing you with adequate exercise, avoiding exposure to extreme temperatures, and addressing any health issues that may arise in a timely manner.

When it comes to living responsibly with other pet owners, maintaining an empathetic and respectful attitude is essential. Every owner has their own style of raising and educating their dogs, just like us. Recognizing that every dog is unique and that there may be differences in how they interact with other dogs will help avoid unnecessary conflict.

It's also essential to be aware of local rules and regulations regarding pet ownership. This involves keeping our Bulldog on a leash in public spaces, collecting their feces and respecting restricted areas for dogs. By doing so, we are demonstrating our commitment to the community and helping to maintain a clean and safe environment for everyone.

In conclusion, the English Bulldog plays an important role as a pet in society. It is our responsibility to promote respectful and responsible coexistence with other pet owners, promoting proper socialization, understanding the needs of our breed and maintaining an empathetic attitude. By doing so, we can fully enjoy the company of our Bulldog and contribute to a harmonious coexistence in our community.

In the second half of this chapter, we will continue to explore how to promote respectful and responsible coexistence with other pet owners, focusing on the importance of communication and mutual respect.

Clear and effective communication is critical to avoid misunderstandings and conflicts with other pet owners. When we meet other dogs and their owners, it is important to be attentive to the communication signals that our Bulldogs are sending, as well as to the signals we receive from the other dogs. If our Bulldog shows signs of discomfort or stress, it is important to take steps to ensure his safety and well-being, removing him from the situation if necessary.

In addition, being respectful of other owners means giving your dog's space and time to get used to each other. Some dogs may need extra time to feel comfortable interacting with other dogs, so it's important to be patient and understanding. Not all dogs want to play or interact right away, and forcing situations can lead to unnecessary stress or conflict.

It is also essential to respect the decisions and preferences of other owners regarding the interaction of their dogs with ours. Some owners may prefer to keep their dogs on a leash at all times, for a variety of reasons, such as behavioral problems or health conditions. It is essential to respect these decisions and to ensure that our Bulldog is under control at all times.

In the event of a conflict with another pet owner, it's important to address it in a calm and respectful manner. Trying to resolve any differences or disagreements through open, non-confrontational dialogue can help find mutually satisfying solutions. The main objective must always be the well-being of our dogs and the promotion of a harmonious coexistence among all.

In addition to communication and respect, it's also critical to take responsibility for our actions as pet owners. This involves collecting our Bulldog's feces in public spaces and making sure that it doesn't cause discomfort or harm to others. We must also comply with local rules and regulations regarding pet ownership, such as keeping our dog on a leash in places where it is mandatory.

Finally, we must remember that owning an English Bulldog in society is a privilege and a responsibility. We must act as ambassadors for our breed, promoting a positive image and educating others about the unique characteristics and special needs of our Bulldogs. By doing so, we will contribute to a respectful coexistence between all dog breeds and to a more understanding and empathetic society towards our furry friends.

In short, to promote respectful and responsible coexistence with other pet owners, we must focus on clear and effective communication, mutual respect, and take responsibility for our actions as owners of

English Bulldogs. By doing so, we will be promoting harmonious coexistence among all members of society and contributing to a better understanding among dog lovers.

Chapter 18: Stories and Testimonials from English Bulldog Owners

Learn about real experiences of English Bulldog owners and how this breed has enriched their lives and family relationships.

The testimonies of the owners of the English Bulldog reflect the deep connection that can be created with this unique breed. Their endearing personalities and unconditional loyalty have left indelible marks in the hearts of those who have decided to share their lives with these adorable canines.

María, a single mother of three children, tells us how the arrival of her English Bulldog, Bruno, completely transformed her life and that of her family. From the moment Bruno entered their lives, Maria experienced renewed calm and joy. Bruno's playful energy and affectionate disposition created a harmonious environment in the home. The children benefited from Bruno's company, and the relationship between siblings was strengthened by their shared love for the English Bulldog.

Pedro and Marta, a couple who recently retired, found in their English Bulldog, Lola, a reason for joy in this new phase of their lives. With her presence, Lola filled the void left by her children when they left home. Long morning walks and quiet evenings in the garden became the most special moments for Pedro and Marta. Lola gave them the opportunity to exercise, enjoy nature and, above all, to have faithful and loving company at this stage of their lives.

English Bulldogs also have the ability to be emotional therapy for those suffering from anxiety or depression. Ana, a young university student, found in her English Bulldog, Max, a source of comfort and support during difficult times. Max's calm presence and willingness to listen without judgment allowed Ana to overcome emotional obstacles. Max became his confidant and a motivator to continue his educational journey.

Another notable aspect of English Bulldogs is their adaptability to different environments. Santiago and Laura, an adventurous couple, have traveled all over the world accompanied by their English Bulldog, Rocky. From mountainous landscapes to paradisiacal beaches, Rocky has enjoyed traveling with his owners. With his fearless spirit and love for exploration, Rocky has been a faithful companion on each of Santiago and Laura's adventures.

These are just some of the stories and testimonies that reflect how the presence of an English Bulldog can enrich our lives and family relationships. Their unique personality and unconditional love teach us the true meaning of loyalty and provide us with a company full of love and happiness.

The connection that is created between the owners of the English Bulldog and this unique breed goes beyond the physical, it is an emotional and spiritual connection that transcends time and distance. The testimonies of those who have shared their lives with these adorable canines show us how their impact has been profound and lasting.

Carmen, a middle-aged woman, tells us how her English Bulldog, Maxi, became her companion during a difficult time in her life. During his battle with an illness, Maxi was by his side, providing him with unconditional support and constant joy. Her sweet gaze and willingness to be close to her gave her strength and helped her to face every challenge. Maxi became their courageous warrior and their greatest source of inspiration.

The stories of English Bulldog owners also reveal how this breed can make a difference in the lives of the little ones. Juan and Laura, a family with two children, tell us how their English Bulldog, Toby, has become an adventure companion and a confidant for the children. Toby accompanies them in all their antics and is always willing to listen and comfort them. The bonds they have created with their beloved English Bulldog have taught them lessons of love, patience and commitment.

The story of Mario, an elderly man, shows us how English Bulldogs can fill our hearts with joy in lonely moments. After his wife's departure, Mario found solace in his English Bulldog, Bruno. Bruno became his faithful companion, providing him with companionship and unconditional love. Every day, when he woke up, Mario found in Bruno's eyes a reason to smile and face the day with strength.

The stories of English Bulldog owners are endless, but they all have a common denominator: these exceptional canines enrich our lives and family relationships in a unique way. Their presence teaches us the importance of enjoying every moment, of rejoicing in the little things and of valuing the unconditional love they give us.

In short, the testimonies of the owners of the English Bulldog show us how this breed can bring joy, companionship and unconditional love to our lives. Whether through difficult times, as sources of inspiration or as companions on adventures, English Bulldogs have the ability to transform our lives and create lasting bonds. They teach us important lessons about loyalty, love and commitment, reminding us that the true meaning of having a pet goes beyond having a simple companion animal. The English Bulldog becomes another member of the family, a faithful friend and an unparalleled gift. Let's keep celebrating and appreciating the wonders that these adorable canines bring us every day.

Chapter 19: The Aging of the English Bulldog

Understand the physical and emotional changes English Bulldogs can experience in their old age and how to provide them with proper and loving care.

English Bulldogs are known for their unique personality and friendly character. Over the years, these adorable canines become inseparable members of our families. However, just like humans, English Bulldogs also go through the aging process. In this chapter, we will understand the physical and emotional changes they may experience during this stage of their lives and how to provide them with the proper care and love they deserve.

As an English Bulldog ages, it's common to see changes in its physical appearance. Their coat, once lustrous and soft, can become duller and less dense. You may also notice gray spots on your face and body, indicating the passage of time. In addition, their activity is likely to decrease and they will become less energetic to play or run. These physical changes are natural and part of the aging process.

Aside from physical changes, English Bulldogs can also experience emotional changes during old age. Like older people, they may show less interest in activities they once enjoyed and may become more withdrawn. You may notice that they sleep more and seem less enthusiastic. This doesn't mean that they are sad or depressed, but rather that they are adapting to the changing needs of their body and mind.

It's crucial to provide them with the right care at this stage of their lives. A balanced, high-quality diet is essential to maintaining your health and well-being. Consult your veterinarian for specific recommendations regarding your English Bulldog's diet during old age. They may need a lower calorie, nutrient-rich diet to control their weight and maintain a strong immune system.

In addition to adequate nutrition, it is essential to provide them with regular exercise adapted to their needs. Although they may show less energy, they will still need to move to keep their muscles and joints in good shape. Take short, gentle walks, avoiding strenuous exercise that could harm your health.

Don't forget that English Bulldogs also need regular visits to the vet during old age. These screenings will detect medical conditions at an early stage and provide them with appropriate treatment. In addition, your veterinarian can help you adjust your English Bulldog's diet and activity level according to your age and individual needs.

As we provide them with the necessary care, it's also essential to show them love and emotional support. English Bulldogs are sensitive and respond positively to the attention and affection of their owners. Spend time petting them, talking to them softly, and allowing them to rest close to you. Their companionship and warmth will provide them with a sense of security and emotional well-being.

In this first half of the chapter, we explored the physical and emotional changes that English Bulldogs can experience during their old age. We have highlighted the importance of adequate nutrition, regular exercise, veterinary visits and emotional support. This care will help improve their quality of life and ensure that they enjoy a healthy and happy old age.

So, now that we have understood the challenges that accompany the aging of English Bulldogs, let's move on to the second part of this chapter, delving into the common diseases that may affect them at this stage and how to manage them effectively. Let us be prepared to face obstacles and continue to provide love and care to our beloved life partners. As we move through this stage in the lives of our English

Bulldogs, it is important to be prepared to face the possible diseases that may affect them. Although aging cannot be completely prevented, we can take steps to minimize the impact of some of these common diseases and provide them with the best possible care.

One of the most common conditions in older English Bulldogs is hip dysplasia. This disease occurs when the hip joint develops incorrectly, causing pain and difficulty walking. If you notice that your English Bulldog is limping, has difficulty getting up, or seems to have stiffness in its hind legs, it's important to see a vet right away. Treatment may include medication, physical therapy, or, in some serious cases, surgery.

Another common disease in old age in English Bulldogs is arthritis. This inflammatory joint condition can be very painful and limiting. If your English Bulldog shows signs of stiffness, lameness, or refuses to walk, it's essential to seek the advice of a veterinarian. Treatment may involve pain medication, physical therapy, and dietary changes to help control inflammation.

In addition, older English Bulldogs are prone to respiratory problems because of their distinctive facial structure. Nasal stenosis and brachycephalic syndrome are conditions that can affect your breathing. These problems can worsen with age, making it difficult to breathe and cause problems with exercise tolerance. If you notice that your English Bulldog is having breathing difficulties, it is essential to go to the vet to receive adequate treatment and avoid serious complications.

Vision and hearing loss can also be common in older English Bulldogs. If your pet seems to have trouble seeing or hearing, it's important to adapt their environment to ensure they are safe and comfortable. You can use tactile and verbal cues to communicate with him and maintain a calm, familiar environment to avoid confusion and stress.

At this stage in the lives of our English Bulldogs, it is essential to pay special attention to their dental health. Periodontal disease and plaque build-up are common in older dogs and can lead to tooth loss and pain.

Regularly brushing your English Bulldog's teeth, using chewable toys and scheduling regular veterinary dental cleanings will help keep their mouth healthy and prevent future problems.

In short, old age brings changes and challenges for our English Bulldogs, but with proper care and attention to their health, we can help them enjoy a full and happy life at this stage. Remember that love, patience, and emotional support are just as important as physical care. By providing them with adequate nutrition, exercise adapted to their needs, regular veterinary visits and emotional support, you'll be ensuring that your English Bulldog ages healthily and surrounded by love. Enjoy every moment with your faithful friend and build unforgettable memories together.

Chapter 20: The Legacy of the English Bulldog

Reflect on the lasting impact that the English Bulldog can have on our lives and how their presence leaves a legacy of love and joy in the family. Pet owners understand the depth of the bond that forms between them and their adorable four-legged companions. But there's something special about the unique personality of an English Bulldog that goes beyond the ordinary.

When an English Bulldog chooses us as his family, an indescribable connection awakens. Their friendly and affectionate character envelops us, and we can't help but fall in love with their unparalleled charm. Its rugged, wrinkled appearance and flat snout are simply irresistible. But beyond their appearance, it's their gentle and devoted nature that truly captivates us.

The English Bulldog is not only loyal and protective, but it is also a true member of the family. He is involved in all household activities and is always there to provide comfort during difficult times. Even on the darkest of days, their warm and friendly presence reminds us that we are never alone. Its cheerful essence fills our home with laughter and happiness, turning even the most everyday moments into memorable ones.

The English Bulldog's unique personality also leaves a lasting impact on our lives. Their entertaining antics and their ability to cheer us up at a glance give us a different perspective on life. They teach us to value small moments and to live in the present without worrying about the past or the future. His presence is a constant reminder of the importance of enjoying every moment and of loving unconditionally.

In addition to its positive influence on our lives, the English Bulldog also has a special impact on our hearts. His unconditional love transcends any barrier and moves us deeply. Their unwavering loyalty inspires us to be better human beings, to seek kindness, and to cultivate relationships based on love and respect. They teach us that the true essence of happiness lies in the selfless love we offer to others.

But this legacy of the English Bulldog goes beyond our own family. As these wonderful dogs become known to the world, their impact extends to other individuals and families. They become ambassadors of love and joy, demonstrating that happiness is found in the company of a loved one, regardless of appearance or race. Through their presence, these adorable canines touch the hearts of those who know them, leaving a legacy of love and happiness every step of the way.

The English Bulldog is much more than just an adorable pet. It is a special being that transforms our lives and teaches us invaluable lessons. In this first part of the chapter, we have reflected on the unique personality of these dogs and how they influence our lives. But much remains to be discovered about their legacy and the memorable moments they bring to us. Join us in the second part of this chapter, where we will explore the unforgettable moments, we spent with these beloved canines. United by unconditional love, let's continue to discover the wonderful legacy of the English Bulldog. The second part of this chapter immerses us in the unforgettable moments we live with these beloved canines. Every day with an English Bulldog is full of laughter, fun and unconditional love. These wonderful dogs find a way to brighten our days even in the darkest of times.

His entertaining antics provide us with moments of endless laughter. Whether it's chasing their endless tail, trying to catch a ball with their flat snout, or clowning to get our attention, English Bulldogs always find a way to make us smile. Their playful nature reminds us of the importance of enjoying life's little pleasures and finding joy in the simplest things.

But not only do they cheer us up with their antics, they also provide us with comfort when we need it most. In times of sadness or stress, our English Bulldogs are there to offer us their warmth and unconditional support. Just cuddling up next to us or giving us a sympathetic look, they comfort us and make us feel loved. They are masters in the art of listening attentively and being present in difficult times, reminding us that we are never alone on this path called life.

Our English Bulldogs also teach us valuable lessons about the importance of loving unconditionally. Their unwavering loyalty and ability to forgive and forget inspire us to be better human beings. They teach us that true love does not judge or discriminate, but that it accepts everyone as they are.

Every day of our lives with an English Bulldog becomes a precious gift. Their eyes full of tenderness and their gaze full of love constantly remind us how fortunate we are to have them in our lives. That indescribable connection that forms between us and our English Bulldogs is unique and enriching.

The legacy of the English Bulldog isn't just limited to our family. As these precious dogs become known to the world, their impact extends to other individuals and families. They are carriers of love and joy, leaving an indelible mark on those lucky enough to know them.

The English Bulldog teaches us to value every moment, to live with joy and to love without conditions. They are special beings that change our lives forever. Through their legacy, they show us that love can transform any circumstance and that true happiness lies in the bonds we create with those we love.

In conclusion, every day with an English Bulldog is an opportunity to grow, learn and love. These wonderful dogs teach us important lessons about life and provide us with unforgettable moments full of laughter and tenderness. They are the guardians of our hearts and ambassadors of unconditional love. Let's continue to embrace the legacy of the English Bulldog and celebrate the love and joy they bring us every day.

Disclaimer

The information provided in this book is for general informational and educational purposes only and is not intended as a substitute for professional advice, diagnosis, or treatment. The author and publisher have made every effort to ensure the accuracy and reliability of the information provided within these pages, but they make no guarantees, either express or implied, regarding the content's completeness, accuracy, or applicability.

Neither the author nor the publisher shall be held liable or responsible for any misunderstanding or misuse of the information contained in this book or for any loss, damage, or injury caused, or alleged to be caused, directly or indirectly by any treatment, action, or application of any advice discussed in this publication. The statements made within this book are not intended to diagnose, treat, cure, or prevent any disease. Readers should consult with a qualified healthcare provider for medical advice tailored to their personal circumstances.

The views and opinions expressed herein are those of the author alone and do not necessarily reflect the official policy or position of any agency or company. All content provided in this book is on an "as-is" basis and the author and publisher disclaim all responsibility for any errors or omissions.

Don't miss out!

Visit the website below and you can sign up to receive emails whenever Gonzalo Estrada publishes a new book. There's no charge and no obligation.

https://books2read.com/r/B-A-OZBBB-DCHZC

BOOKS 2 READ

Connecting independent readers to independent writers.

Also by Gonzalo Estrada

Self Healing
Visualiza tu Éxito
Cultivando Líderes
Afirmaciones y Empoderamiento
Semillas de Cambio
Cómo convertir TikTok en una máquina de hacer dinero
Cómo hacer dinero con Pinterest
Cómo hacer un ensayo
Cómo Pedir un Aumento de Sueldo
Currículo Poderoso
Entrenamiento sin Violencia
Entrevista Laboral
Gana Dinero con X (Twitter)
Ganar Masa Muscular
Volver a Empezar; el arte de reinventarse
Analiza Resuelve Ejecuta
Aromatherapy, The natural path to your pet´s well being
Holistic Feeding
The ABC of Educating Your Pet
The Art of Cosmic Connection
The Art of Feng Shui applied to your Pets
From Scarcity to Abundance
The English Bulldog in The Family
Therapeutic Massages for Pets

www.ingramcontent.com/pod-product-compliance
Lightning Source LLC
Chambersburg PA
CBHW051250160726
47994CB00003B/1102